Sown

Rooted in Redemption

K. PRICE

978-0-578-70670-2

Table of Contents

ROCK

Away	9
Kief	11
Afraid of the Dark	12
Prude	13
The Prayer Garden	14
Blue Hot	18
Legs Day	19
Airplane Cake	20
Goulash Recipe	22
Valentine's Day	23
Spring Break	24
What Happens in Vegas	25
Killer T-Cells	27
Summer School	28
Fight Club	30
The Boy With the Benz	32
Last Chance	33
She	34
I'll Make You Hate Me	35
Left Side	38
Mother	39

The Angel's Prayer   41

Ocean Angels   43

Chocolate Chip Waffles   44

Vodka Sauce   46

Trooper   47

She   48

Cancelled   49

My Sheol   50

Rainbow Jawbreakers   52

Mother Knows Best   54

Wanderer   56

Hemochrome   57

Lipstick Legs   59

THORN

Silver Fixation   62

Night Church   64

Angelique   66

Europe   69

The Mediterranean   70

The Girl on the Bus   71

Barcelona   73

Trans-Atlantic   74

Church   75

Come to Me	76
Echo Rings	78
Pick up the Phone	80
The Call	81
Blackout	82
What's Left of Me	84
Who I Am	86
Our Father	87
Leftovers	88
Lifeguard	90
Cover Your Ears	91
Summer Love	92
Apple Ale	93
Nostalgia	96
Tree of Life	97
Lungs on Fire	98

SOIL

Mark 4	102
Her Name	103
Redeemed	104
PTSD	105
In Time	106
The Last Time	107

Fast Daydreams   108

Profession   109

Holy Waters   110

ROCK

I crash into the water fingertips first. Followed by the top of my head, my shoulders, my hips, and then my toes. Splash! The sound of underwater, a sudden *swoosh* in the drums of my cap-covered ears. My heart is pounding, and under the water, it is my beat. I don't even notice the bite of the chilly water because my skin is so flushed with anger. I have goose pimples underneath my arm hair. Why do I do this to myself? I should've just listened to my roommate. She's always right. I wish I could swim away from here, just settle into a nice little nook on a seastar. Not a starfish, a seastar: as if there were a galaxy under the water like there is in space. Because if there were such a place, that's where I would want to live. Under the water, away from the rest of the world. Just... away.

Away

I used to swim for you.
Every Tuesday, every Thursday,
we used to leave for lunch after—
soon I went alone.

I let out my anger to the water.
All of my pain.
The lapping waves
were my blood.
I was letting you out.

Twice weekly
I drained myself.
Every time I took a breath
I saw you looking at me still
and swam faster

until I cramped,
crying out in the middle of the lane:
visible pain,
so you could see my hurt,
feel it outside my body.

Inside wasn't enough.
You had to see what you'd done to me,
why I leeched onto you for so long.

The water is blue for me now,
Bluer than it's ever been before.
Your spot closed three times over.
I let all of you out.

I met Zaid at orientation. Actually, I shared a table with his friends and mine. It was later on I became friends with Zaid, at our job at the pool. He was cool, though. It was a breakthrough moment, finally finding someone who smoked too. So I have my people, like usual. My smart people and my party people. I'm set.

In this new environment, university, I was excited to pave my own way, make my own rules. It was exhausting, creating my own world, but once I found my niche, everything started making more sense. Class, class, sleep, club, repeat. Monday through Thursday, then nine to midnight, up early for work at the pool, sleep, drink, smoke, repeat.

This, I could get used to.

Kief

Stuffy and dark—
sun bursts open and lights up my day.
Fingers' rigid whorls awaken me,
stirring my daily routine.
Fingers massage me from head to toe;
then pierce me, slice me,
expose my innards. Every day.

Fingers scatter dust on me from above,
pinch me, pack me,
caress me all over.
Dancing under slithering clouds,
lips lap up the fairy dust from the corners of myself.
Fingers set fire, igniting my bones.
Exhale deeply and release the stress.

Let me quiet your mind as you
take a bored breath.
Lick your fingers—
pick me off your tongue.

Afraid of the Dark

I woke one night,

        looked at the end of the bed:

        A figure loomed.
        Eyeglass-less,
        it was blurred,
        but stood as tall as
        the ceiling fan,
        one dimension,
        no face,
        as though a black
        curtain hung at my feet.

I hid my face from its presence
under the sheets.

        Jesus,

                if you're real,
                rescue me.

Prude

I ask Roomie
about the little book she wakes up to read.

Her bible is so tiny,
compared to the one
that hides under
anatomy
books on my nightstand.

Roomie,
what does it mean when you say
"God, one in three?"

He's the Father, He's the Son,
He's the Spirit.
One of three, three in-one.

The Prayer Garden

There is a little prayer garden
next to the chapel
I like to visit
if I'm not too hungover.

I sit there and think
between cigarette puffs.
I call my high school boyfriend
to break things off.

I daydream about Zaid,
when I'll see him next,
or I sit down there after
jogging, to catch my breath.

I sit there on Sundays
for weekly family talks.
I stand by the bushes
for pre-clubbing photos.

I claim a seat there
filing cards for
anatomy class.
I go there to study
before occasional
Sunday mass.

The prayer garden
is beautiful,
perfectly versatile.

The prayer garden
has definitely become
my favorite altar.

I walk downstairs to the twelfth floor. Tucked into the back corner is his door. Zaid and I, our friendship is unique in a way even I can't understand.

Tonight is the night. I could sense there was something growing in between us months ago. Tonight, we will stay up until dawn peeks out behind the treetops, before I leave for swim practice. Tonight I'll set it all out on the table and tell him what's on my mind.

There is shame that entangles itself in our bond. There is disgust for the way I find myself facing his front door again and again, giving pieces of myself, but getting nothing in return. No hand-holding, no definition, nothing.

It's late this evening. We turn off the TV, and I settle into the spare bed, too tired to walk up the stairs to my own. I take a deep breath, muster the courage to ask. I say it simply.

"Are we, you know, a 'thing?'"
"No. I'm not allowed to date. No, we're not a 'thing.'"

Plain as day.

I take a deep breath while my heart sinks and grieves. I don't leave, though: I stay huddled to his side even after his emotionless reply. How could he not be aware of the way our souls were entangling? The guilt that will follow behind me in the morning when I leave for the pool will be too much to bear. I know I will return to the corner room as though I'm missing out on something I know won't satisfy our appetites. The way he manipulates my attention-seeking spirit is fine-tuned, even though his hands are rough to the touch and his words abrasive to the soul. Why I come back, I do not know.

Our friendship is unique. I pretend that the more I give of myself, the more likely this will become the real thing. Zaid pretends he isn't addicted in the worst way. I pretend that he won't lead me on. He pretends that he isn't forcing me to consent. Our friendship is unique.

Blue Hot

My anger burns platinum blue.
It's the hottest part of flame,
the bottom, a fluorescent hue.

The rejection sears through
me from my bushy eyebrows
to my narrow feet.

I can't focus.
The hours I wasted
bother me.

Anger pulsates through
my veins.
I'm craving self-destruction
I need release.

Legs Day

The way that rejection stings
makes me desperately crave release.

I find my trusted lane and dive in.
I don't take a breath for three lengths.

I punish myself in the water.
I kick until I cramp.
I curl up like an eel—
zing!
My quadricep throbs.
I have to hold my breath
to float and bob,
nursing my aching leg,
the water hides my sobs.

I scream under the surface
where no one can hear me.

I desperately need a release.
This rejection stings.

Airplane Cake

It was just the cake
on his face
I come to realize,
after a recording
and vomit stain
fill me in the next morning.
Where is my suit?
I woke up facing a fan.
Before that was black.
Before that was stairs.
The disfigured man.
...if you don't
want to dance,
then say no.
No.
Come to my
bedroom.
Bedroom?
No,
I need the
bathroom.
Bathroom.
"Goodbye so-and-so,'"
the green icing said.
I was the hottest girl in the room;
the hot tub left me warm and confident.
Screwdriver.
The guys there wanted to dance with me
in my borrowed Columbia
zipped over my bikini.
There were guys
making my
screwdriver.

I had to dance away my pain.
Tequila shot.
I saw strobes from the hot tub.
Felt the bass underwater.
Where there is music,
there is beer.
It was February.

Goulash Recipe

I broke the spine of an American Girl
book. On the cover, the only variance:
their height, skin color.

I looked at mine,
disgusted with myself.
Beauty is not colorblind.

The way I would grow,
bullet points from
a book
would become check-boxes
in my journal.

The stuffing and then
the fasting
began to excite me.

The gnawing of my visceral cavity
fighting its civil war.
I was fighting a war with
empty bullets,
empty bowls.

The last supper:
I flipped to a new recipe.
A first try at goulash
in a spotless apartment.
Porcelain never looked so pearl.
I stained it burgundy with tomato sauce
and chyme.

Valentine's Day

She wore a little black dress
with little blue triangles
tipping over the scale of ugly.

Zaid introduced me to this nameless girl
in her awkwardly high heels.
"We were on a double date."
I stood in the dorm lobby in my sweats.
No Valentines for me.

I stared at this poor girl.
You don't know what
you've gotten into.
My mind tells me he is mine,
but just because I visited his door
a few nights before,
doesn't save my spot
on this unorthodox
roller coaster.

I want to tell this nameless girl
that her triangle tips overlap.
I could certainly do it better.
Instead I turn and leave.
Happy Valentine's Day to me.

Spring Break

I'm ashamed to say what I let happen
on spring break.

A group of us escaped
to the hills of Oklahoma.
Campfires, music, a few
drinks.

Roomie warned me against it—
but I invited Zaid.

This is my last chance
to have a good time.

School is down my back—
I'm falling behind.

Zaid is the last thing
I need right now,
but I can't help it.

One last visit won't
hurt me.
I know I'm addicted.

What Happens in Vegas

He's the bullet in my chamber
and I'm playing Russian roulette.
With my eyes shut,
with my left hand
spun around three times,
counting in cards.
He's the ace to my spades,
the one to my twenty,
my jack, my die, my penny slot.
I wait for the sevens to line up—
I keep pulling the pin again and again,
entranced by the thrill of our game.
Your grandness ceases to die,
I play our numbers more and more.
My chances are slim,
yet still my pockets overflow.
There's something caffeinating my soul.
I can't say if it's your shiny lights
or empty seats that keep me engrossed.
I'll keep coming back and filling up on you,
as long as we don't reach the last shot.

The night I noticed her, we were sitting under the bunk bed, trying not to touch knees. She wore a low braid; I wore a bright yellow sweater, and my owl shirt underneath.

I felt the flap of the grey and brown wings of that owl shirt against my flushing cheeks, hearing its hoot reverberate inside my skull like the sound of the popping ping-pong balls against the solo cups in front of the bed.

When I saw you, I was dancing, laughing, not drinking. I know you remember the yellow sweater, but do you remember the owl sitting behind you? I'm sure you noticed I was afraid to get too close, so the owl kept its distance. I'm sure you felt its presence, too.

I was trying so hard not to touch your knee with mine.

Killer T-Cells

Out of nowhere,
I'm slapped
with desire.
The crevices and craters
left of my memory
and the plica folds
in my gut,
encourage urges
that feel like they are
appearing
out of thin air.
Pain surges to the
tips of my
fingers—
don't touch!
I fight my own flesh
to suppress.

Innocence forsaken
for forbidden,
momentary thrills.
It kills me every time
I think about it.

Summer School

I wake up in my quiet campus apartment,
sun radiating through my blinds.

Wake, dress, eat.
I prepare for chemistry.

Bike, park, lock.
Note-taking; the lecture goes on.

Gym, home, knock.
I take a glance at the clock.

Hoot.

It's the girl with the braid
from the dorm party.

We've become friends—
her summer school's just starting.

She tells me about the crazy ex
she's trying to make amends with,

punches walls with frustration,
asks if she can stay until my date's here.

I make her an ice pack
to rest her bruised hand in.

You can stay.

I say,
You can stay.

Fight Club

I go to fight club every
Wednesday.
I know my problem
wants to steal my identity.

I can't help the urge
of not wanting to keep
food down,
and my drug of choice
gives me heavy delusions.

I sit on a couch,
she sits in her chair.
Tell me, why do you
think you are here?

There's a boy,
I tell her,
who's broken my heart.
Everytime I let him in,
my life continues
to fall apart.

I go to fight club
in the middle
of the week.
I tell the lady how I
constantly crave
something strong to drink.

Stay away from that boy,
maybe things will get

better.
See you next week,
take care.

I leave more bitter.

The Boy With the Benz

I took a risk with
the Boy with a Benz.

His attention caught my eye.
I bet myself I can make him mine.
I just want someone who wants me, too.
The Boy with the Benz has the time.
In the gym mirror,
I thought I caught his attention
with my eyes.

He took me out one summer night.
The breeze through my hair
felt so good, so right.
Top down, music on.
I was sure,
I had that Boy with the Benz.

Weeks later, in my confidence,
I send him a text.
"I can't tell if you like me, too…"
A flutter ran through my
skinny gut.
I already know what he'll say…

"I'm sorry, I didn't know
you had feelings for me."
That definitely wasn't it.

Last Chance

He was my last chance,
that Boy with the Benz.
Something must be wrong
if I couldn't even lasso him.

I read that message, then looked up.
The girl with the braid sat deep in thought,
waiting in a pose too serene,

his reply, so unexpected.
My self esteem in smithereens.

I read the message aloud to the
girl with the braid,
and maybe it was actually a spell.
As once I cleared the tears from
my eyes, I saw a halo lived around her skull.

But I wasn't done with the Boy with the Benz.
I had a wedding to take him to.
So he became my cover.
She saw my wounds
and wrapped them clean,
telling me she understood.

He was my last chance,
The Boy with the Benz,
but maybe he lead me
to new happiness.

She

The owl perched itself on the
pitch-black window sill.
Where underneath sat my
overnight bag.

The moon shone through the window
and her red pillowcase laid beside my head.

She was my everything.
I lost myself in the curls of her hair,
Her giant eyes—
She.

I'll Make You Hate Me

It's been two weeks
since the wedding.
My cover was blown after
the Boy with the Benz
left in the middle of dinner.
"I have friends waiting for me at the bar."

I look at the guests across the table,
try to hide my embarrassment,
take my cousin for a cigarette.
"I'm a lesbian, okay. Don't say anything."

It's been two weeks since the wedding.
I stumble to my front door,
still drunk from the party earlier.
I opened her phone while she was
passed out. Saw she was texting
her old girl still.

It's been two weeks; there's no way
I'm giving up yet.
She told me she'd stick
by me until the end.

"The next girl I date,
I'm going to make my wife."
Two weeks doesn't compare
to the rest of my life.

"I'm telling you know,
I'll make you hate me."
She was promising to break

my patched-up heart.
It's only been two weeks.
This is just how it starts.

This all makes sense. All the rejection. It's because I'm just not meant to be with boys and men. The curiosity that flared in me when I found those adult magazines. It's because for me, it's clearly not meant to be. I remember the man at the bookstore, in the children's section with his shorts too short. His smile full of malice, my innocence shrieking in self defense. It was setting me up to one day see that boys just weren't meant for me.

Left Side

I forgot how good it felt
to be enveloped under heavy arms,
folded against long legs.
Her wrist curled over my clavicle.
She searched for my hand and held it,
taking me by surprise.

I held it back,
and she separated each finger as though
picking petals off
a daisy. I helped before she
made it to my pinky, hooking it under hers.

I can't tell if it's embrace I'm addicted to,
or words. I've left you so many times before.
Like magnets, we make it back to this embrace,
and again, I beg you to stay.

In a moment's hesitation I question my
sanity, as it seems
you've been my devil all along.
I hang onto your every word
just as I hang onto your pinky finger.

Mother

My mother came
to see me.

I showed her
my new things.

*You better not
have anyone else here,*

she states
with a face of fear.

I show her my new
grandfather sweater.

You like it?

I tell my mom
summer school is
"going."

I can tell she's
not listening.

*You better not
let anyone live
in this apartment.*

I show her my
latest thrift store find.

She's onto something,
I can't tell what.

I feel like you're
letting someone
in this apartment.

Mom, lay off.
I distract her again.
Why the boy clothes?
Are you gay?

I say *no*
without a doubt.

The Angel's Prayer

Now I lay me down to sleep,
and after my prayers my secrets I keep;
hidden inside throughout the day,
let themselves out to come and play.

I've never stolen a single heart.
I don't understand how it's a fault;
kindness.
She tells me *kindness is a weakness.*
The owl begins to hoot—
listen to her, listen to her.
Trade your smile for a scowl,
that's better, that's better.

The click of the fan above my head
ticks off the time that I spend
scheming how to catch her in the act.
What are you talking about?
She demands. *I said I'll be right back.*

Our owl wakes me at 7am on the dot.
Hoot hoot, through the trees, here she comes,
the owl teases.
From where she's come,
I don't know,
but the trees see everything.
I know they know.
My mind clicks like the fan,
an overheating machine;
that's cooling me off while I sweat
in my dreams.

Devils, mine don't come out just at night.
Mine crave the day and even twilight.
When sleep takes my idle mind,
and binds mind-blowing memories back to life,
All I can think is how I'm awful,
I'm awful, I'm a slowly sinking brick.
But my devils can't drown me
since they know how to swim.

My eyelids shutter, trying to stay closed.
Our owl hoots louder, *She's here, She's here!*
I'm faking my sleep, so she won't know
that I've been watching the window
since she left home last night.

With her red pillow case and our owl ,
I watched them take flight.
"I'm sleeping at my place tonight."

Hoot, and break, hoot, a break.
Okay, whatever, I said.
But once she left, I saw where she went.
She walked through the trees across the lawn,
Then circled back, once she felt she was far.
Hoot!
Then she walked two apartment buildings away.
Hoot!
Her old girl dropped her scan key through the gate.

Ocean Angels

I cast my last hopes
into a vast ocean
of despair.
I've lost myself
in her,
in my lusts.

I baited my eternity
on the end of a hook.

I cast my rejection
into an ocean of
idols.

There are few things
that numb
my pain,
my hunger.

What is left to catch?
I've lost myself in ocean angels.

Chocolate Chip Waffles

Hips hurt.
Knees hurt.
Ankles hurt too.
More bruises than ever before:
wanting to be soothed.
Can't reflex, won't reflex.
Can't toothbrush,
no fingers.
Have you ever felt the back of your throat?
Bubbles, grumbling, pains.
There are no number milestones to
meet anymore.
Lovely carbs are all I think about.
I told myself my toothbrush is only for my teeth,
I've got to keep them clean,
after purging chocolate chip waffles.

I haven't been to the pool since Halloween. She doesn't like me going there because she doesn't trust Zaid. He and I haven't talked since we fell out after spring break. I work there once in a while, but I don't bother to swim anyway. It'd kill my legs.

Vodka Sauce

Let me cook tonight,
she offers.

We visit the store:
chicken breast,
penne noodles,
vodka sauce,

in the red pot
with the red spatula.
It tastes so bland.

After some time,
I choke down
the meal to
appease her.

Let me cook tonight,
she offers.
I want to say no.
I always want to say
no.

I let her cook again.
Same old vodka sauce,
Same old red pot.

Trooper

Periwinkle wrinkles
make their way
into every seam.

Troop 994,
the shirt reads.

The threads pucker and pull
and loop back around,
over and around and crossing again—

threatening to unravel
at the neckline.
A deep wave pulls it down
towards my clavicle,
anything but sweetheart.

The color of periwinkle
chokes me.
I can't breathe.

She's my living hell,
and my vision starts
to fade from the pressure
against my neck.

She

She is all I could ever need.
My partner—
when the world turns against me,
She is there.

You may ask,
am I okay?
That, I cannot say.

She is all I need.
I can't tell,
I won't listen—
it's between us.

She says she's all I need.

Cancelled

I stopped going to fight club.
She says I don't really need it,
that she's the best therapy.

My Sheol

My Sheol has milky, milky,
periwinkle walls.
Thick, dripping, falling into puddles
of purple paste.
Sunflowers are plastered to the
pukey surface.
They are revolting.

Milky, milky purple.
Muddled slow jams
ebb through
periwinkle paste dribbling
down the wall.

The music never stops—
it offends my ears.
My skin, it makes crawl,
my stomach begins to quease.

I can't get out of this hell.
I look for a way out,
but instead I find my altar
with its photo of a peek-a-boo
tattoo.
It's a giraffe: its eyes are enormous.
From its frame,
it stares at me, unblinking.

I made my own Sheol,
picked the color by hand,
selected the music accordingly,
marked my territory with my own blood.

My walls could have been
endless sky
with her nowhere in sight,
but I chose milky periwinkle.

Rainbow Jawbreakers

It's pointless to brush my teeth
if I will still wake with
that bile taste in my mouth.

Regret stuck in my gums.
Depression hanging from my palate.
Foul sour film over my tongue,
the residue of broken morals.

The sugar's already seeped into my bloodstream.
I had the chance to spit out the putrid sweet,
but those curves were like hard candy.

I had to taste it, I couldn't resist.
I wanted to know what
surprise was waiting inside.

I should've known unwrapping it
would open Pandora's box.
I should have known that was
only the beginning of temptation.

Eight deceitful suckers I kept tucked
in my cheek.
They made me vomit.
They made me bleed.
Caused my stomach to twist into knots
and my heart to race.
The side effects bubbled green and purple pain.

I kept on biting through them, though—
sacrificing my teeth to a bittersweet crunch.

Even when they left me choking on the living room floor.
They tasted just like the strawberry shells
I used to steal from the grocery store.
They made me sick with guilt,
but still I ate, and braced my neck to crack number eight.

Mother Knows Best

I went home to see
my Mother.
I took *her*, too.

We acted casual,
acted nonchalant,
"We're just friends,"
we practiced in unison.

I went home to see
my mother,
and made a mistake.
Someone saw us
kiss when
we thought they weren't
looking.

I went to see
my Mother,
she called me
into her room.

I know what
you did.
Now's your chance
To talk.
Are you gay?
You need to
tell me,
or you need
to get out.

Yes.
Yes I am.
There, now you know.

Well then, she needs
to leave,
or you both need to go.

I call up a ride,
and pack up my suitcase.
Mom, we can't separate.

She tries to stop me,
tears cascade down her face.

I take one last look
at what I'm leaving behind.
I look at my lady
and see death in her eyes.

Wanderer

My owl t-shirt hung
wrinkle-less
from her old girl's hanger.

My eyes glazed over with red—
I followed the pattern of their
footsteps a few hundred feet away.

Hoooooooot.

I had to know what was happening
behind this window screen.
"That's what you get for being curious,"
she tells me.
I grab the owl by its neck, snatch it towards my chest.

Its feathers flail in its distress.
HootHootHoot!

I leave with a knot in my back
from the angled doorknob.
I reach out trying
to reclaim our owl.

I grab it back, its beady eyes
popping with fear.
I stormed out with my owl t-shirt
drenched in my tears.

Hemochrome

A spear made just for me,
it came in a blue plastic sheath.
The metal inner-tube glimmering,
reflecting the brown fingers holding it,
reflecting a brown thigh beneath it—
dragging, slowly, counting,
one... two... three...

When burgundy appears, slowly it tears,
crying a red somber shade.
When it smudges, it sticks
like war paint.
One, two, three
horizontal stripes
decorate my sinewy thighs.
They are little pieces of death,
but they make me feel alive.

I haven't seen Roomie in weeks. Once in a while, when I can manage, I visit her over breakfast. She doesn't care for my braid-clad babe to come along, and it's not often I can manage to shake her off. I can tell she notices the gradual sink to my eyes. I just try not to make contact. *How are you?* she asks. I don't bother with the truth because one, *she* is right here, and two, I know she's going to bring up God and stuff. So I say, like usual, *I'm fine, and you?*

Lipstick Legs

My thin legs hang over the arm of the loveseat.
My eyes flutter open,
roll in their sockets for a moment,
lipstick still in place.

Our favorite show flashes across the television
screen and the apartment smells like eggs.

I peel my lipstick legs off the tiny couch,
still wet from this morning's rain.

I haven't heard a word from her, since she left.
She said she's not coming back this time.

I answer the knocking at the door:
not her, but a friend, holding a bottle
of hardened tears to replace
the ones I've already spilled.

Soon, the tiny apartment
smells like cinnamon
and a creamy tonic
is passed my way.

Liquid cinnamon rolls
down my throat
into my coin pouch
stomach.

My eyes start
rolling back again,
but it feels so much better—

this time I'm about
to take off.
My mind starts to
spiral like the swirls
on a cinnamon bun.
Finally
the numbing begins.
"I've got an idea,"
my cinnamon breath
says for me.

It's $15 Tuesday.
Let's get pierced.
In my head,
I say "that will show her
I can't handle pain."

We don't bother with umbrellas
as we trample through
puddles, piling into a tiny car.

The pain comes through
a thick needle,
a pin drop of blood leaks.
For a second, I feel redeemed.

I stand up from the table,
but the feeling washes
over me again.
Shame and sadness flood my veins,

my cough tastes like cinnamon.
I confidently stumble back
to the tiny car.

She took her things
when she left the tiny
apartment, and though
it's only been a day,
the open spaces
already feel normal.

My lipstick legs
drape over the tiny couch.
Rain patters,
the door knocks.

She bursts into tears,
asking to come back in.
I should say no,
but my cinnamon
breath tells her yes.

THORN

Silver Fixation

I wear a silver chain
with a silver cross that hangs
against my sternum with hope.
When I'm worried, on it I grope.

It's an outdated idol,
yet I wear it every day
as though to absolve
the things called "sins"
with which I like to play.

As I walk to my daily death—
the arms of my lover,
the cross dangles and thumps
against my heart and my sternum.

It's an outdated idol,
I say in my head.
Yet, I still hopelessly pray
it provides me protection. today

Night Church

I want out.
I hate her, truly,
I do.
I want out.

It hit me out of nowhere,
the guilt of how far I have strayed
into my own cycles of destruction.

I've come here a few times before with Roomie,
so I know the directions.
I sit in the back of what I'd usually call pews.

I listen for what feels like an eternity.
I wait for an opportunity to see
the pastor, in his jean pants...
what is this night church nonsense?

I ignore my judgement, and stand in line,
"Pastor, do you have the time?"
We sit in the pew, so I can pour out my heart.
I can barely gauge where to start.

I want out. This is my limit.
I want out—
how do I do this?

He listens intently, with compassion
so deep.
He flags down a woman,
her name is Angelique.

She approaches,
I sense wisdom in her soul.
Angelique, this is K.
Come listen,
because I must go.

She sits down beside me.
I sense she is safe,
so I begin to speak.
her gaze is intense.

Now she's weeping
with me—
what on earth did I do?
Dear girl, I'm so sorry
what's all happened with you.

Angelique begs me,
Please meet me next week.
At a coffee shop,
bring *her* if you must.
Do whatever it takes.

Angelique

A stud and a fem walk into a coffee shop.
With her Clarks boots and boy pants,
it almost takes a second glance to
notice the femininity of her jaw
and how petite *she* is.

A stud and a fem walk into a coffee shop.
I scan around the room for Angelique.
It hardly takes a second glance to
notice the glow surrounding
her long blond hair. She

stands to greet the stud and the fem,
and gives us a tight embrace, looks
me straight in my face. I'm so
happy to see you, and you
as well. Come, sit down.

A stud and a fem walk into a coffee shop.
Hypothetically, she explains, *after*
you have warmed up. She opens
the door and you trail behind.
You cross the street, then
are struck from behind.

If a stud and a fem left this coffee shop,
And were struck by a car, died on
the spot. Where would you go?
Well, to heaven of course.
By what standard, what
means? By what accord?

I'll tell you this now, with love in my heart,
if you stud, and you fem, were struck by
a car, your sins would keep you far
from the heavenly throne. By
Christ's blood only can
you fully be atoned.

Not your mothers, not by baptisms,
not by faith alone. You have to
accept Jesus, let him live on
your throne. He'll ask you
to end this. You think
you can do it?

I want him, how I want him,
yet I don't think I can
go through with it.

Today's six months. For winter break, I share the holiday with my estranged family. The tension is overwhelming, and I'm not even staying with my mother. I have Christmas dinner with our close friend: she happens to accept the outcasts, and now, I'm one of them. My lady is in Hawaii with her family; her mother is getting married. It's the only state that allows gay marriage. I only have to stick out this separation another week before we meet up again. One more week. Before my trip to Europe, she's taking me to her hometown. We'll celebrate our six months over New Years fireworks. Meeting a milestone for once makes all the pain worth it. I can forget my meetings with Angelique. Six gruesome months with my lady.

Europe

My aunt drops me at the
entrance to my gate.
This is the ultimate escape.
She can't follow me here,
I feel guilty as I think,
I'm not even upset I left
on the tail of our
six-month-aversary.

She can't follow us here,
hoot hoot.
I feel like this is the tail end
of this relationship.
An ocean to divide us
after our anniversary trip
could do us good.
If she can keep her word.

I saw the messages—
it was her old girl again.
She can't follow me to Europe.
Surely she'll give up her tirade.
Six months of threats against me.
In Europe nothing could
stand against me.
An opportunity to start clean.

I walk through the entrance to my gate.
This is my big break.

The Mediterranean

Hoot, hoot.
I turn my gaze from
the vast green-blue sea.
It's our owl, it's here,
it's got something to tell me.

I bring my eyes back to
this once in a lifetime view.
Not now, not now,
still I hear
hoot, hoot.

I look down at my phone,
he points his beak to a blue bird.
I press on it and suddenly
my world unfolds.

"My baby is back,"
the message is brief.
I look at our owl.
She's been cheating on me.

The Girl on the Bus

I have a bad feeling about this—
the last seat available
is next to one of the girls
from night church.
She keeps a smile
plastered on her face.
I tried to avoid her
except for when Roomie
would stop to talk to her
and I would be forced
to smile back at her.

I sit next to her,
see if my lady has
messaged me back.
The headphone trick
won't work on this chick.
She gets right to it.

"I was hoping you'd sit by me."
This Jesus freak?
Now this ride is going
to get bumpy.
"I saw you at night church,
what do you think?"
I explain how I'm just
looking into things.
I'm going through a lot
and wanted some guidance.

The Rosary and the hymns
never did much for me,

I explain,
so I came to night church.
There's something there
I can't deny,
that makes me feel
whole inside.
Even when my lady
comes along,
no one stares.
I thought it was something
you people were strictly against?

This girls face brightens up,
we've got three hours to kill.
Let me tell you all about it.
And for some reason
I relax and sit still.

Barcelona

I'm standing
up above this city
that I've been hoping
to see and explore,
yet I cannot ignore:

this isn't as marvelous
as I thought it would be.

Trans-Atlantic

I met God in Europe.
He showed me
how far I'm racing.

He met me at the Great Sea,
sent me that message
so I could see
how my sins will keep
following me.

I tried to get away,
wanted to break away,
God, help me find a way.

I met God in Europe.

Church

I'm going to church today,
you coming or not?

She ignores me
and continues to lay
down in our bed.
I shrug and continue
getting dressed instead.

The girl from the bus
lives in the apartment across.
I scale the stair flight
and meet in our parking lot.

I sigh—it's a deep
breath of relief.
It feels so good to
get away from
everything.

Come to Me

Weary, burdened wanderer,
there is rest for thee
at the feet of Jesus
in His love,
so free.
—**"Come to Me"**
LAUREN CHANDLER

For the first time,
I open my mouth to sing.

I'm used to quiet church,
counting along on a rosary.

The guitarist starts to strum,
the room gasps together.

I introduce my voice
and feel lighter than a feather.

This song,
it feels like it was
written just for me.

It says,
there is freedom, taste and see.
It lures me deeper
when we all sing,
Come, oh come to Me.

I need rescue, I need release,
Come, oh come to Me.

Tears are flowing, I can't believe...
Come, oh come to Me.
There is freedom,
I've had a taste.
Come, oh come to Me.

Your burden carried,
He will take,
Come, oh come to Me.

Echo Rings

Get off me, get off me,
I'm trying to keep my voice
from echoing.

I'm done. I want out. Get off me.
She grabs me,
slamming me down
near the sink.
Her fist winds up,
drawing back.
Her eyes are pitch black.

Get off me.
She grabs me,
pushing me down.
I hit the towel ring
and my back starts to throb.
I scuttle to a stand,
I run for the door.

In my fear, I manage
to crack it open.
Get back inside she says.
I hoarsely say, *No.*
She holds me by my hips,
I beg her to let me go.
Get off me, I breathe,
I take off her promise ring,
throw it down the hallway,
where she'd have to release
me to reach.

Dinggg,
dingdingdingding.
She lets me go.
Her eyes are still
blacker than night,
I leave and hear
the sound of my ring
down the hallway
still echoing.

Pick up the Phone

I'm going to kill myself
if you don't come back,
she tells me breathlessly.

I have your ring.
If you want it,
come back to me.

I squeeze my eyes tight,
and think of
the King.

Pick up the phone.
No.
I say,
I'm leaving.

The Call

I call two girls, saying
I need to tell them everything.
Over a chicken sandwich
I can barely touch,
I spill out to them my entire heart.

Every message,
every picture,
every behind the scene.
We had no idea, they'd tell me.

Blackout

Hoot hoot

Not today. I shut the blinds
and turn up the tv.
I open a warm beer
though it's nine in the morning.

Hooooot

I drown out the sound
with another swig,
shuffle nervously over
to a space at the sink.

Under my jewelry box,
hides a blue sheathed piece.
I hold my breath tight
and open my release.

Hoot

I turn off my phone,
I climb back in bed.
I leave bloody tracks,
and take another swig.

Hoot hoot Hoot hoot
LEAVE ME ALONE.

I open the blinds.
Our owl thinks it's

arrived home.

She's not here anymore.
She's gone back to her
old girl.

We don't want you anymore,
it's time that you go.

The silence is deafening,
only the click of the fan.
The room is finally spinning,
so I open another drink.

My disclosure of the abuse
gives me a free pass from class.
I saunter around campus
with secret drinks in hand.

Two more days pass,
my legs become a treasure map.
When the alcohol runs dry,
I finally take a step back.

The silence is deafening,
between my ears on autopilot.
I sober from my walking slumber—
it's time I fully break my silence.

What's Left of Me

Our relationship eroded the confidence
that once shone in my eyes.
For brief moments I can smile.
Then, the memory of my willingness
steals away any joy I had left.
Somber is now my daily emotion.

What I manage to recognize through hazy eyes
is the way the sky still manages to make me smile.
I have become so content in my willingness
to take part in my own self destruction—what's left?
I dare not raise my chin, I'm sold out by my lack of emotion.
What is confidence?

I try to separate my lip from the other to form a smile.
Barely do they part, as the willingness
to exert such a force saps what energy I have left.
I cannot express emotion.
Only a whisper escapes my throat. I had confidence
someone would have listened to my eyes

and see my willingness
to change. To turn left.
To muster what emotion
I can manage, what confidence
remains, what my eyes
have seen. How much I miss my smile.

There is not much of me left.
She was a leech that lived off my emotion.
The fake confidence
reflected in her high eyes
over her fake smile
overtook my willingness.

Abuse is an emotion
that steals the confidence
of those who once lived with open eyes.
It buries smiles,
absolves willingness,
leaves the victim to gather what's left.

Fear is the emotion, read my eyes.
Hold onto your confidence, what willingness
is truly left. Petrified, I simply smile.

Who I Am

Girl,
do you dare lift your head
as to hope?

Why bother?

I will only pull you
down by your
disgusting chin hairs,
bowing your head
to shame and sorrow.

Inadequate,
miserable,
failure—

Satan.
That's who this voice is.
What is it that you want with me?
Have you not taken everything I had
to give?

Was it you?
Why do you tell me these things?
As though I'm not low enough.

Inadequate, miserable, failure,
There must be more to me
than that.
There has to be.
Please, let there be.

Our Father

Pray then like this:
"Our Father in heaven,
hallowed be your name."
　　　　　　—**MATTHEW 6:9**

I can only
swim
so fast
with this
soul
that is drowning
in unfamiliar
sorrow
and angst
that only
you
can fix.

Leftovers

I look for help in all
the wrong places.
I go to fight club
every Wednesday,
trying to make sense
of every mistake.

I want to be whole again.
I still look for help
in all the wrong places.

I go to fight club twice a week now. I want so badly to continue the destruction, but my soul cries out. Zaid walked me to it recently. He says he's glad to have me back. I know I should probably just stay away from him, but I can't help it. I can't help but take him back.

Lifeguard

The tile is cold
against bare feet.
My airless head
bobs
to the corner of the pool

where I lower
myself
into deep waters
that envelop my earlobes
and pang the back
of my throat,
making me want to gag.

Zaid watches me get in
and sink to the bottom.
Rescues me,
slides me up to the side of the pool
again,
straps me to a board,
where I have to lay paralyzed,
as he winds me against
dry wood,
and then clasps my head tight,
my eyes still misty,
while I'm still choking on water.

He thinks he can save me,
but I'm far from lost.
He wants to come as my rescuer.
However, I'm unworthy of rescuing.
Even from his dull sword and rusted armor.

Cover Your Ears

I am drawn by Zaid's pretty words,
strung together with silver silk webbings
entwined with dishonesty.
His pattern yields a contortion so mesmerizing
that every syllable leaves a track of desire along my arms
in the form of goosebumps.

His pretty words glisten on the tip of his tongue
that can wrap its way around my mind and hold on tight,
structure sentences into promises so convincing.

Crooning, comforting to the ear.
I'm here for you.
Take off the rose-tinted glasses, I want to tell myself.
Embrace those pretty words as though they are just that;
billowy bursts of air.
The air has the ability to turn back time and open pages of an old
story.

Summer Love

I forgot what it felt like
to have a hand a little bigger than mine pressing into my palm.
Not too soft...
I forgot what it felt like
to hear a bass voice singing along to the radio
not faking having to sound deep.

Apple Ale

My red lipstick won't fix this one.
This puzzle I'm struggling to piece together—
the pieces don't want to fit and I'm shoving them into place.

Red lipstick smudged by the end of the date revealed my
humanity.
Lord forgive me,
for I have sinned
out of lust.
Beautiful, horrible, shameful lust.

Three

10pm—
the witching hour.
My kickback can start.
We round in a circle,
stereo on the perfect playlist.
Door tap,
bottle cap,
Crisp.
The gang's here.

11pm—
we round the circle,
stereo drones on,
perfect playlist bass
bumps in tune
with the lighter snaps
and bottle caps.
Crisp,
shwhoooo...

12am—
we trail down
the stairs,
sneakers shed,
shorts on,
hop the fence
to the hot tub,
Shhhhh...

1am—
the party stops,
tired and high.

Zaid hangs back,
we follow old habits
back to the bed.

Three years
He denied me of
this moment that
our souls
would collide.

The sun rises,
my alarm blares
obscenities at the foot
of my bed.
I wake,
my footsteps
quieted by the carpet,
I can't deny what I've lost.

Nostalgia

You brushed my hand and the flashbacks hit me like a fierce wind.

I had a year to mull over my mistakes, the feelings left in room 1208.

I wake up next to you and still don't mean a thing.

Tree of Life

For all have sinned and fall short of the glory of God...
—ROMANS 3:23

I took off swinging,
hanging from rope
too thin.

Stranded between
landings, a low hiss,
threads unraveling.

Losing a grip on life—
dangling.
Help!
Threads popping,
snapping,
I fall.
I reach out
for the landing.

Tree tops beneath
catch me.
I clutch them,
bring chilled lips
to bumpy bark,
whispering
thank you,
thank you,
thank you.

Lungs on Fire

> *He said to them, "Because of your little faith.*
> *For truly, I say to you, if you have faith like a*
> *grain of mustard seed, you will say to this mountain,*
> *'Move from here to there,' and it will move,*
> *and nothing will be impossible for you."*
> **—MATTHEW 17:20**

I remember the first hit better than my first kiss.
It was only supposed to happen once. It became my answer to
everything:
a deeper sleep, a need to eat.

Better not to have to think at all, yes?
Let the world revolve without you, yes?
Feel your alveoli pop with every sweet pucker
kissing a fresh blunt, oh yes.

Much better.
My mind—
My mind is, numb:

that nameless, empty space
between being a paralytic
and a vegetative state.
I filled it with smoke. Yellow,
horseradish mustard-colored smoke.
so heavy it took my eyelids
for the ride too.

But, the thing about smoke is,
it condensates, or
evaporates. It hastens

the soul's disintegration.

The bottomless haze makes life feel fuller.
Blurred eyes burning but lids can't lift more than a sliver.
Breathe out enough and it's all gone.
Then there's nothing...

Horrifying, nothing replacing
something, or someone specifically.
He, who captures the darkest
souls with light the size of a mustard seed.
A miniscule dot navigating through space
and combusting into its own cosmos.
From one seed-size prayer you can
become one with the universe again.

Not from the buds
of the ground, but from the love
of a Savior. Oh,
how wonderful to be blinded
by a light so consuming.

A light that kindles a fire from the inside out,
leaving you awestruck.
There is an answer to nothingness
that works, that stays.
All it takes is to breathe Him in.

SOIL

My legs are tired after the bike ride from work. My skin still burns with the leftover glimmer of sunshine. My swimsuit is plastered to my tinted skin. I collapse on the couch, flipping around the screen. Nothing. Nothing to watch. No one's home. No more joints. No company. Nothing. I opened the heavy, leather-bound book. Picking up where I left off before I moved from my apartment a month ago, I couldn't afford the rent. My mom let me move back in. I miss the car I only had for three weeks. Sylvester was what I named it. I'm left riding my little brother's bike to my high school job. It's not my pool at school, but this old one will do for now. Day in and day out. No friends, no drugs, no parties. I open up the heavy book to where I left off…

Mark 4

"Whoever has ears, let them hear, "
Let them hear?
"...like seed sown on rocky soil,"
With these mystery words I sit and I toil.
Let me see, please,
make it clear to see.
Suddenly
the skies open up
before me.

MY DAUGHTER—

The voice is loud and near.

My daughter,
don't you see?
My daughter,
don't you hear?

In my sun-faded suit,
sweat still stuck to my back.
I collapse by the couch,
drenched in the Holy Spirit.

Her Name

She tore me apart
hair by hair,
skin cells lost in
tormenting friction.

Microscopic portions of
my soul, stomach, heart,
flatlined and went septic.
I was left a shell that no
longer could echo the sea.

I did my part in shaving away
the few barriers she had left standing.
Insensitivity came to run
my once compassionate soul.

My only hope
for her is to see the rich
holiness that has repainted
my insides.
My happiness is yet to be found,
but in me love at least resides.

Redeemed

> *...giving thanks to the Father,*
> *who has qualified you to share in the*
> *inheritance of the saints in light.*
> *He has delivered us from the domain of darkness*
> *and transferred us to the kingdom*
> *of his beloved Son, in whom we have redemption,*
> *the forgiveness of sins.*
> **—COLOSSIANS 1:12-14**

This guilt has no hold on me—
it's been swept away
through skin pierced on a tree.

My Redeemer,
my everything.
Her name no longer
means anything to me.

PTSD

I'm left with fragments that
freeze me in mid-step.

No creeping, no whispering,

don't touch my neck.
or kiss me behind my ear,
or lift your arms too high,

or cook with vodka sauce,
or play slow jams,

and please don't wear Clarks.
Or wear fishtail braids,
or that cologne,

no Camaros, please don't buy me a rose.

I hate sunflowers,

I don't want to hold hands.
I don't want to get too close.
I'm just learning to trust again.

The fragments that form me
are very incomplete but
they are all I have left,
in my world with PTSD.

In Time

For I know the plans
I have for you,
declares the LORD,
plans for welfare
and not for evil,
to give you a future
and a hope.
—JEREMIAH 29:11

In time
I'll be made
whole.
I'll wake up
and the sound of owls
won't make me bawl.

In time I'll be made whole.

The Last Time

It's Friday night, I need a release.
I've got a plan, I'll only have one drink.
It's been quite some time since I've seen Zaid,
I'll bring a friend this time
so she can tell me when to stay away.
Contrary to plan, one drink turns into five,
I need to go to the bathroom,
my friend helps me inside.

This time my mind swims with
liquor and shame.
I know by coming here I made a mistake.
We leave the bathroom to meet up with Zaid,
We barely make it down the staircase.
Go back! Go back!
The police are storming up the stairway.
We backtrack into the apartment,
slowly close the door.
God is surely with me,
I feel it in my core.

After a night of close calls,
I've finally hit a wall.
I'm done playing back and forth.
I'm ready to be in this full-force.
The morning brings a unique surprise,
my head doesn't ache with the sunrise.
My God, my Rock, Mighty Hand,
forgive me, forgive me,
thank you for one more chance.

Fast Daydreams

What we hunger for most, we worship.
—**JOHN PIPER**

A dwarf rose in hand, I saunter,
to a place in the breeze I can ponder.
Word vomit dry-heaves from a diet of only water.

Twelve months ago, I was rapidly approaching a hell,
the stench of a past, thank God I forgot the smell.
Instead, in my newfound life, I dropped sin in a well.

I ate a last supper of saucy stew. Later came sleep,
to give up human nature to Him without a peep.
Like His forever, my promise I will keep.

For today, I will not eat.

Profession

Go therefore and make disciples of all nations,
baptizing them in the name of the Father
and of the Son and of the Holy Spirit,
teaching them to observe all that
I have commanded you.
And behold, I am with you always,
to the end of the age.

—MATTHEW 28:19–20

I want to have a proper profession.
As I'm not an infant, I want to do it again.
I tell Mother and Father—
they are worried and hurt.
I let them know that I'm not going to desert.
I've changed, this is good, you have no need to worry.
My profession of God's goodness is part of my story.

Holy Waters

I stand in a shallow pool.
Under the hot lights,
I sweat to keep cool.

The faces before me
show a glimpse of heaven
on earth.
I stand reading my story
at night church.

Roomie is with me,
we say our rehearsed line—
Do you believe God,
three-in-one,
the only Divine?
I nod, and she proceeds
while slowly leaning me,
then I baptize you,
Father, Spirit, and Son,
let this water
show you are clean.

Made in the USA
Coppell, TX
28 June 2020

29496556R00066